RADIANT SHARDS

Copyright © 2020 Ruth Panofsky

Except for the use of short passages for review purposes, no part of this book may be reproduced, in part or in whole, or transmitted in any form or by any means, electronically or mechanically, including photocopying, recording, or any information or storage retrieval system, without prior permission in writing from the publisher.

The publisher gratefully acknowledges the support of the Canada Council for the Arts and the Ontario Arts Council. The publisher is also grateful for the financial assistance received from the Government of Canada.

Front cover photograph: Courtesy Jewish Heritage Centre of Western Canada
Back cover photograph: Courtesy Archives of Manitoba

Cover design: Val Fullard

Library and Archives Canada Cataloguing in Publication

Title: Radiant shards : Hoda's North End poems / Ruth Panofsky.
Names: Panofsky, Ruth, author.
Series: Inanna poetry & fiction series.
Description: Series statement: Inanna poetry & fiction series
Identifiers: Canadiana (print) 20200203363 | Canadiana (ebook) 2020020338X |
ISBN 9781771337571 (softcover) | ISBN 9781771337588 (epub) |
ISBN 9781771337595 (Kindle) | ISBN 9781771337601 (pdf)
Classification: LCC PS8581.A644 R33 2020 | DDC C811/.6—dc23

Printed and bound in Canada

Inanna Publications and Education Inc.
210 Founders College, York University
4700 Keele Street, Toronto, Ontario M3J 1P3 Canada
Telephone: (416) 736-5356   Fax (416) 736-5765
Email: inanna.publications@inanna.ca   Website: www.inanna.ca

RADIANT SHARDS

Hoda's North End Poems

RUTH PANOFSKY

inanna poetry & fiction series

INANNA Publications & Education Inc.
Toronto, Canada

ALSO BY RUTH PANOFSKY

POETRY
Laike and Nahum: A Poem in Two Voices
Lifeline

NON-FICTION
Toronto Trailblazers: Women in Canadian Publishing
The Literary Legacy of the Macmillan Company of Canada: Making Books and Mapping Culture
At Odds in the World: Essays on Jewish Canadian Women Writers
The Force of Vocation: The Literary Career of Adele Wiseman

EDITED COLLECTIONS
The New Spice Box: Canadian Jewish Writing
The Collected Poems of Miriam Waddington: A Critical Edition
Adele Wiseman: Essays on Her Works

For Liza

*and in memory of
Adele Wiseman (1928-1992)*

Contents

Foreword	xi
Prologue	1
I: Beginnings	3
II: Initiation	25
III: The Lump	53
IV: Afterbirth	67
V: The Dark Time	77
VI: Renewal	97
Coda	110
Notes	113
Illustrations	114
Acknowledgements	115

Hoda really liked love, now that she had found out exactly where it lived and how it worked. Love lived where it couldn't help itself … where it had to be ….

—Adele Wiseman, *Crackpot*

Foreword

Hoda, the protagonist of Adele Wiseman's 1974 novel *Crackpot*, has long occupied my mind. Years ago, she leapt off the page to become a literary companion and now — as a result of my poetic engagement with Wiseman's fiction — she has made her way into this volume.

Radiant Shards would not exist but for Wiseman's creation of a fully formed character and the particular world she inhabits: the Jewish enclave of North End Winnipeg during the first half of the twentieth century. Indeed, readers who know *Crackpot* will recognize the figures and narrative arc of these poems, as well as the liberties taken along the way. And for those unfamiliar with the novel, Hoda resides here, brought to new life.

In Wiseman's fiction, the sex worker Hoda — she preferred the term to prostitute — is presented via a third-person narrator. In my work, she is given her own lyric voice. Occasionally, she evokes the language of *Crackpot*. Always, she speaks in a voice of my imagining. Alternately youthful and mature, this voice plumbs Hoda's private thoughts and tangled feelings. Sometimes, it is directed outward in response to those who would question Hoda's choices and behaviour.

Wiseman claimed to have based her heroine on an actual figure of North End Winnipeg, once home to the city's red light district. Over the course of this project, my admiration for the loving and resilient Hoda — a hybrid of the real, the fictional, and now the poetic — has only grown and deepened.

Toronto, January 2019

Prologue

As I walk
the North End
streets
Hoda's body
the pitch
of her voice
beckon

Soon
I find myself
yielding
to her rare
dignity
compassion
and grace

I: BEGINNINGS

~

No —

I wail
when Mamma dies
the hump on her back
the lump in her belly
weighing her down
pushing her down
into the earth

when Uncle Nate
our unwilling sponsor
threatens to
tear us apart
send Daddy
to the Old Folks Home
and me
to the Orphanage
just because he's blind
and I'm a kid

when Miss Boltholmsup
dismisses me
and my story
vulgar, so vulgar
she sneers

inciting the kids
in class
to the same
humiliating
scorn

when Yankl the butcher
offers soup bones
and meat scraps
in exchange for
a little feel
a hand job
but I do it
anyway
for the food

when Morgan wants sex
lures me to it
with promises of love
and though it feels good
I still whisper
No –

I plead
when David
turns up
at my door
forcing me to choose
between betraying myself
or deceiving him
and so I say
Yes
to my son
as I sob
No

No
David
        No

~

To quiet me
and to show
her love
Mamma offers
roast chicken
potatoes
apples
        and cake

But Daddy's
stories
fill me
like manna
links to a past
that widens
with
        each telling

~

That Boltholmsup
so cruel a teacher –

I face the class
proudly share
my story of
the plague
Rokhl   Danile
their wedding
the great miracle
of my birth.

And what does she do –
gasps   panics
cuts me short
denies my tale
of triumph.

So the kids
laugh and taunt

> *Run, Hoda, run*
> *Hoda weighs a ton!*

and I laugh, too.

What else can I do
to hide the shame
that cuts through me
but slink away
to curse
Miss Beastly
Bottoms-up.

~

        Fatso cow
the kids call me
      cracked too

but I know better –
my body sparkles
my mind stirs

let them jeer –
I say *nuts* to them

~

When baby Malka
dies at birth
Mamma and Daddy
take it as punishment
>	*two grotesques*
for their
arrogant wish
>	*should never*
to give life
raise a child
of their own
>	*have children*

But when the One Above
changes His mind
and bathes my arrival
in Divine Light
>	*an aberration*
they take it as
a different sign –
they too
are people
>	*born to misfits*
who deserve
the blessing
of a capricious
beneficent God

~

Uncle Nate
brought us over
from Russia
and Daddy says
it wasn't easy –
he wrote letters
filed forms
paid bribes.

> *But that doesn't*
> *give him the right*
> *to lord it over us!*

When Uncle barges
into the house
Mamma scurries about
resents the
Charitable Big Shot
for being so
high and mighty.

Daddy gets quiet
is kinder
to his rich uncle
more willing
to accept the
Big Boaster.

I try to behave
show respect
but secretly
I slam my
Snaky
Uncle Nate.

~

Dr Hershfeld
comes by
finds a watermelon
in Mamma's gut
warns

    It must come out.

Too busy
cleaning houses and
earning our keep
Mamma promises
she'll go to hospital

    Later later.

But I know
she's more afraid
of the doctor
and St Joseph's
than the giant
pink melon
seeding
her stomach.

~

When she's rushed
out of the house

writhing
in pain

I shout
Mamma, Mamma

into the scuffle
but no one hears.

Suddenly
there's
silence

and I
hide
under the bed.

At dawn
Daddy returns

to gently
draw me out

into the light
of morning

and the depth
of grief.

~

*Why did Mamma
go and die?
Why did she leave me?
What did I do?*

I am small
I am scared
but no one sees
no one cares.

~

Those Christian ladies
show up to help
but all they do
is snicker and
sneer

> *This house
> is a shambles* and
> *the stew stinks*

> *They're ghastly –
> the fat little girl* and
> *the blind father*

When they leave
I'm much sadder
miss Mamma
so much more

~

Ravenous and
newly renounced
by Uncle Nate

> *You freakish pair*
> *don't deserve*
> *my help*

I visit Yankl
and accept the
butcher's bargain

He gets what
he's begged for
in secret

Daddy and I get
meat for soup
to last the week

~

I mourn Mamma
in my still
small place
of solitude
anguish
piercing
and profound

~

But wait —
here's Daddy
whose stories
will me back
to life's surface and
lead me to the source
the origin
of my great becoming
a tale so epic
it implores me to listen
and concede
yes, yes, I am here
against the redoubtable odds
of history, hatred, ritual
and new loss
I rise again
blessed by my beloved
benign father
a healer

~

Daddy may be blind
but his hands can see
to make
intricate baskets
a skilled craftsman
of grace and instinct
he defies
the insolent taunts
of those
less gifted with sight

II: INITIATION

~

The first time
I wrap my legs
around Morgan
tightly
then tighter
he cries
I love you I love you I love you
words
I need to hear
to do it again
with my Morgo
my dear Morgo

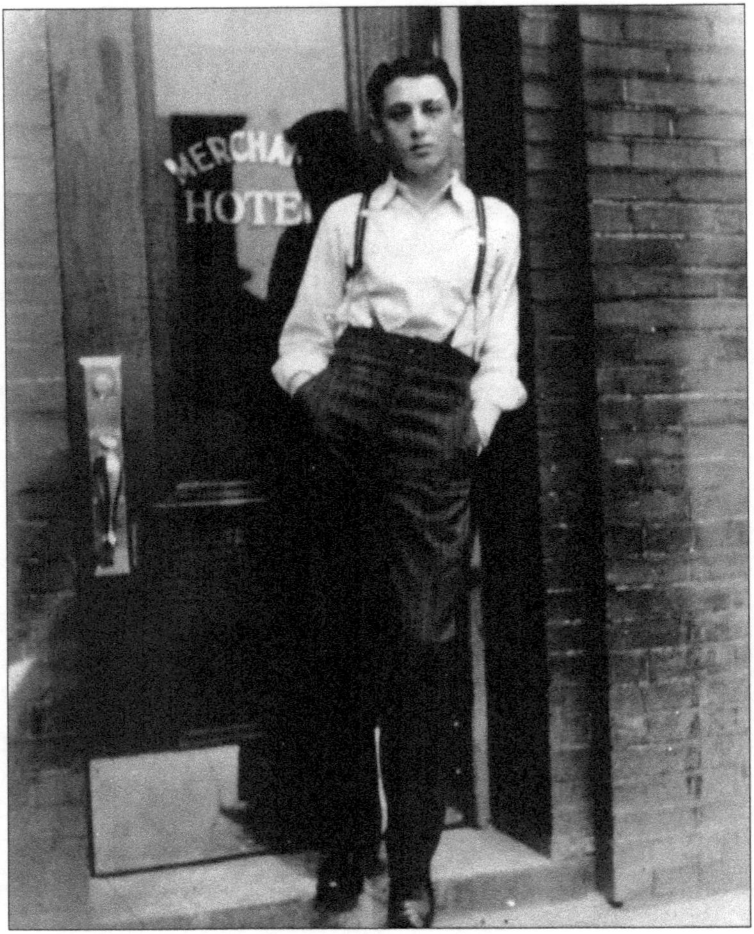
MERCHA
HOTE

~

Morgan
lied

I'm not his
one-and-only

girl
of his dreams

> *You're friendly*
> *funny* and
> *you put out*
>
> *but love*
>   he says
> *no dice*
>   *so long*

~

It starts innocently
without purpose
or plan

visiting boys
come to share
a good time

safe in this
place of ease
we give

ourselves to
big deep
belly laughter

of pain subsiding
in waves
of raucous joy

~

Soon I learn
hard truths

>   never expect love
>   and
>   never give it away for free

they will
climb atop
explore the folds
of my body
plunge
cocooning flesh

>   they want
>
>   they want
>   freedom
>   they can afford

~

They crave
their pleasure
piece

stake a claim on
the *resident*
whore

but when those
artless boys
come to me

I offer
more
than sex

my girth
gives love
takes suffering

~

The Prince of Wales
comes to me
in dreams
of deliverance

He travels
to the North End
rescues me
and claims me

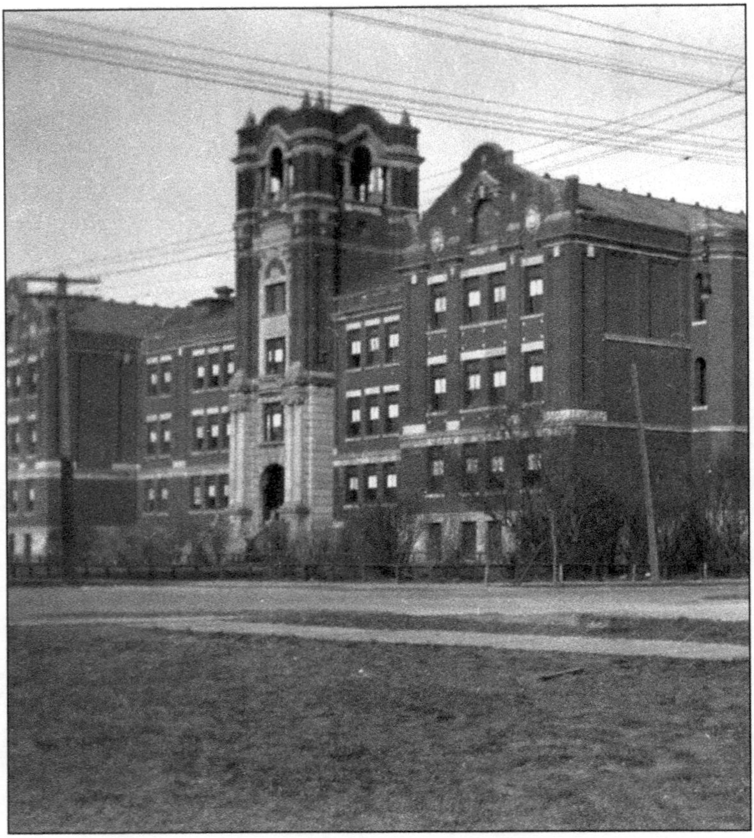

*Hoda, Hoda
big fat cow*

*Hoda, Hoda
she knows how*

*grab her
poke her
climb aboard*

*Hoda, Hoda
big fat whore*

> – Schoolyard chant
> St John's Technical High School
> Salter Street

~

I josh
and joke to
shield a
soft heart
so like
folds of flesh
that let
fellas
in

~

This house
with splintered stairs
sloping porch
and cardboard walls
makes refuge for
the loneliest of boys –
Benjy and Ralphie
Gordie and Hymie –
who seek solace
in swaddling arms
as they moan
in pleasure
and sorrow
a dirge
for their
small lives
and mine

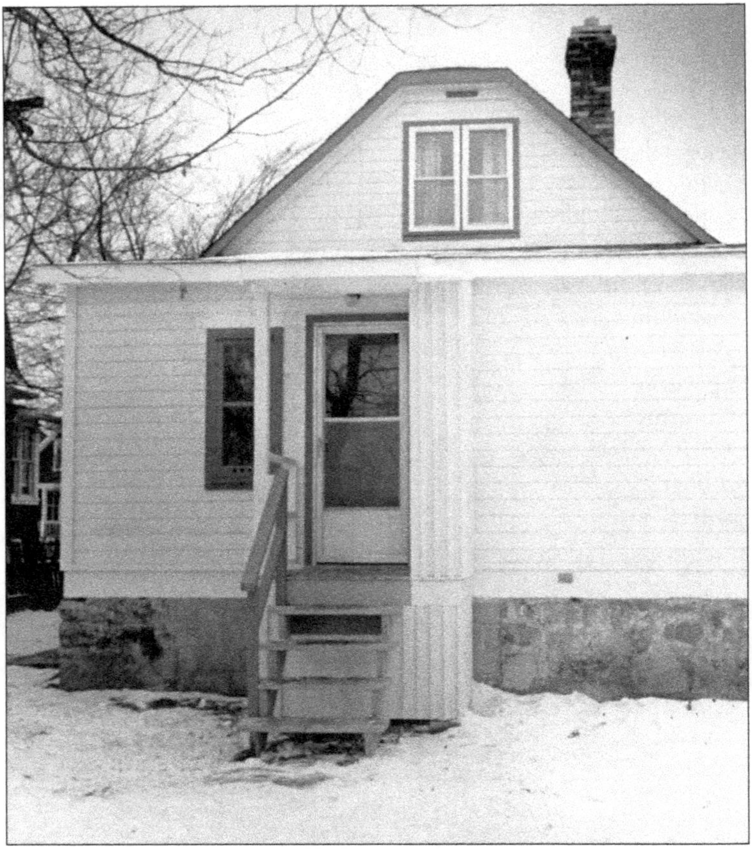

~

Hodaleh, Hodaleh
Daddy calls
his voice

nearly breaks me
he is gentle
I betray his trust

easily
sleep with boys
in the adjacent room

and pretend otherwise
I do it for him
to earn our keep

and make him safe
by my side
in my sight

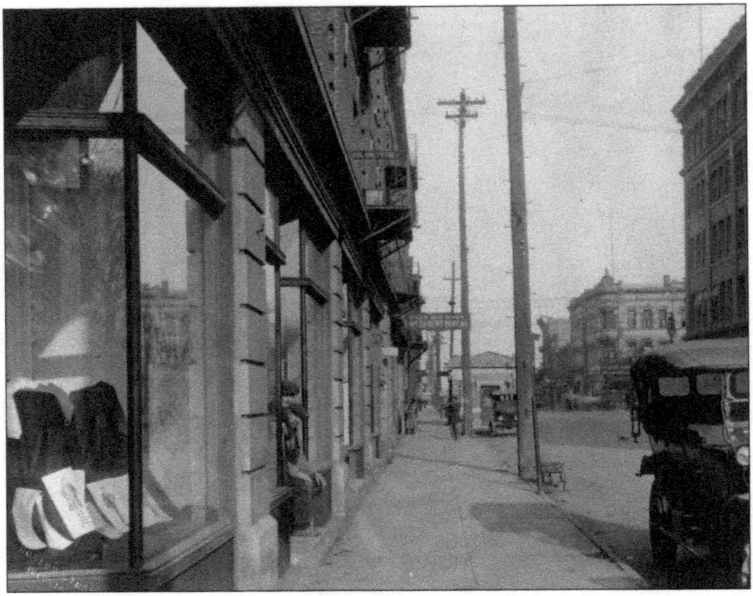

~

Seraphina's
friendly coaxing
finally persuades me
to go downtown.

> *Where's the harm*
> *exploring the city*
> *beyond the stinking North End*
> *meeting some*
> *classy meatballs*
> *making a few extra bucks?*

As it turns out, a lot.

A blackened eye
a beating
I never know
with my boys
who clamour
for their Hoda
romp about and
roll off spent.

My boys
bring me home
to stay.

~

Since her dad took off
Seraphina minds
brothers and sisters
while her ma growls
and whacks

I see through
heavy makeup
and powder
such
sadness
in her eyes

How lucky am I
to have Daddy
so much more
a mother
than Seraphina's
mean old ma

~

I do not judge

never say no
                    blow job
absolutely no
                    gang shag
so they
                    let loose
with
                    good old
cheer on
                    raunchy Hoda

Aroused
boys cling to me

I take them in
hold them close

there is ample room
in the rollicking fun

that brings them
back often to

my place
of reckoning

~

Lewd, you say?
Yeah, I'm lewd,
crude and
coarse, too.

I make my way
with my body –
what else
would I be?

A polite little Sue
refined and lady-like?
No way,
no damn way!

~

I stay local
not a lot
of dough

boys
with odd jobs
have little
to spare

and men
have wives

but Daddy and I
are together
for now
that's enough

~

Those who enjoy

Hoda's Home Hospitality

- ✡ Hand job – 10 minutes
- ✡ Blow job – 10 minutes
- ✡ Body rub and tug – 15 minutes
- ✡ Solo shag – 15 minutes
- ✡ Group shag (maximum 3 boys, 10 minutes each) – 30 minutes

Must also purchase

Danile's Divine Baskets

- ✡ Bread basket
- ✡ Knitting basket
- ✡ Clothespin basket
- ✡ Laundry basket
- ✡ Shopping basket

~

I make a little
on the side
crashing
weddings

At first I go
for the meal
a chicken feast
I can't pass up

But ageing guests
emboldened
by lust and liquor
invite me outside
      for a breath of air
a quickie
in the back alley
against a wall, a tree
in the wood lot
or darkest recess
of the synagogue's
boiler room

The extra money
really helps
gets me thinking
of *the cash*
      to be made
           at funerals
and soon
I'm such a regular
the rabbi will
not intone
until I arrive

~

Commie Polonick
my Yiddish teacher
draws me in
to the fight
for worker's rights

> *And why not?*
> *I'm a worker, too*
> *aren't I?*

I deserve rights
just like women
in factories
bent over
sewing machines

With placards
in hand
they march
the streets
and demand

PROPER WAGES FOR PIECEWORK

> *Hell, don't I know it?*

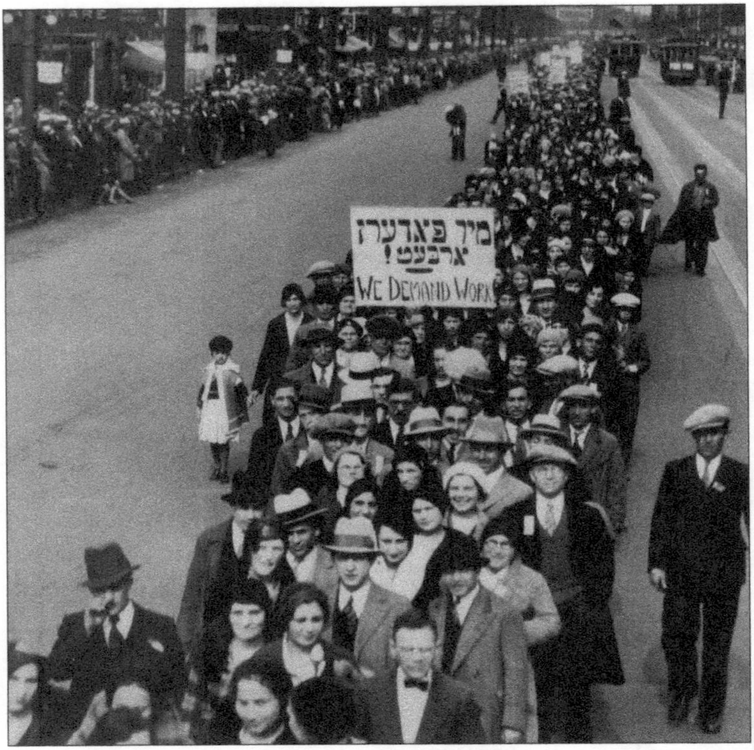
מיר פאדערן
ארבעט!
WE DEMAND WORK

~

Without thinking
I lunge at the Mountie
on horseback his
truncheon raised
for attack

grab his arm
bite down hard
and give
such a shock he
drops the club
falls off the horse

instantly
I'm revolutionary
a local hero
of the striking
masses

III: THE LUMP

~

At Yankl's butcher shop
Mrs Moroznick snorts
*You're as fat
as a cow, Hoda*

*I'd rather be fat
than foul
fishwife*

But when
my stomach
rumbles
and aches

I worry I'm
like Mamma
nursing a lump
in my belly

~

I prod the lump

The lump
scares me

> *Somebody help me*
> *Take it away*
> *Please take it away*

~

I shine
Mrs Minuk's floors
scour her toilets
to scrub
fear

      Cleaning wipes away
      the lump

~

I awake
lump tearing
at my insides

My body
threatens
to implode

~

And then

>			a
>			knife
>			cuts
>			through
>			me

>	again

>	and again

pierces

with such force

>			I burst

>	*What's happening, Mamma?*
>	*What terrible thing did I do?*

and

stops

suddenly

I'm torn

gasp for breath

~

I hear a rustling
in the bed sheets
    What moved?
    What is it?
leap off the bed
to look
but I'm
weighed down
    By what?
bound
by a thick, wet cord
I pull
    pull again
and when it squawks
the lump
    now a baby
    now a boy
I see
birth
break in
darkest night

~

My first concern is
    Daddy
        can't find out
I gnaw
the cord
knot myself
into the fullness
of this black night

~

I survey the scene
        – mattress soaking
        – lump squirming
heed the voice
that urges
        – think later
        – act now
while Daddy
sleeps I
        – heave the mattress
          into the shed
        – wash the lump
          count its fingers, toes
          wrap it in clean sheets
        – stuff more sheets
          between my legs
rush into the night
deposit the bundle
on Orphanage steps
hide
and when the door
opens
                      flee

TAKE GOOD CARE OF
A PRINCE IN DISGUISE

My note
sparks rumours
earns him special care
devotion of the
Director's barren wife
she claims him
names the foundling
David *Ben Zion*
Son of Zion

Interlude I

But the orphans
call him *Pipick*
for his protruding navel
the strange knob left
on his infant body
a sign that he was born
of Hoda's ignorance

How it must wound
to be known
for the numinous nub
that signals
mangled origins
unknown
yet enduring

Interlude II

A crushing sadness
forces Hoda
to seek refuge
in the tub
where despair
cannot be drowned

Can
one body
bear
such loss?

She longs to return
to the darkness
that delivered her son
but Danile won't allow it
tends to her in this illness
rekindles the living
suffering spark

~

If only Mamma
were alive

I'd have
asked about
    body hair
growing in
hidden parts
    budding chest
swelling
aching
    monthly bleeding
awful
cramps
    babies
put by men
into women

At the library
I learn

stark truth
vow privately
    never again, Mamma
    never again

IV: AFTERBIRTH

~

I arrive at
the Orphanage
in a grand limousine
chauffeur driven
to reclaim
my son

        A
        reverie
        that soon
        dims

        unlike
        the living
        breathing
        red-raw night

~

Boys baffled by
my testiness
grumble
Hoda's not feeling so hot

It's my time of the month
an easy answer
to keep them away

Can't let them near me
    Steer clear

Can't bear contact
    Don't touch the goods

Won't heed their pleas
    Forget it   Hands off

~

Daddy's tenderness

> *Hodaleh, Hodaleh*
> *Surely, it can't be that bad?*

nettles me   too

> *What does he know?*
> *What the hell does he know?*

~

Shame   remorse
boil up

but I face
the day

cook   care
for Daddy

beat down
feelings

hard
                      fast

~

I am different   more

a new knowing
carries me one day
to the next and
I welcome the
boys back

they must be quiet
now use rubbers
as I let them
back
in

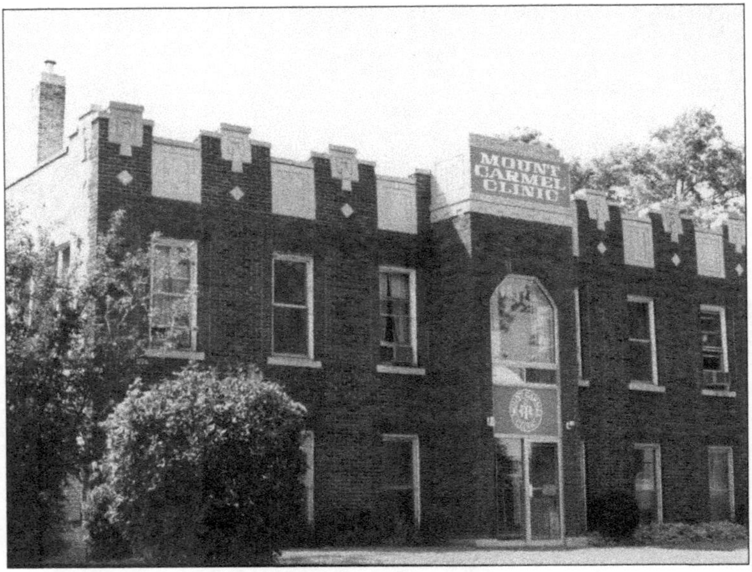
MOUNT
CARMEL
CLINIC

~

In the waiting room
at Mount Carmel Clinic
to test for VD
I turn *kibitzer*

>   *Worried about the clap, are ya?*
>   *Maybe a little bit pregnant?*
>
>   *My line of work?*
>   *Oh, I make ends meet.*

The press
of memory
eased by
banter

~

Polonick tries to
convince me
to stop

> *It's bad*
>   he says
> *What you're doing*

But you ask
Mr Anti-Capitalist
how else to
make a living
he comes up
with

> *Nothing*

V: THE DARK TIME

~

At the double feature
I ponder
romance   love
given freely
like the first time
with Morgan
transported
to a past
with no future

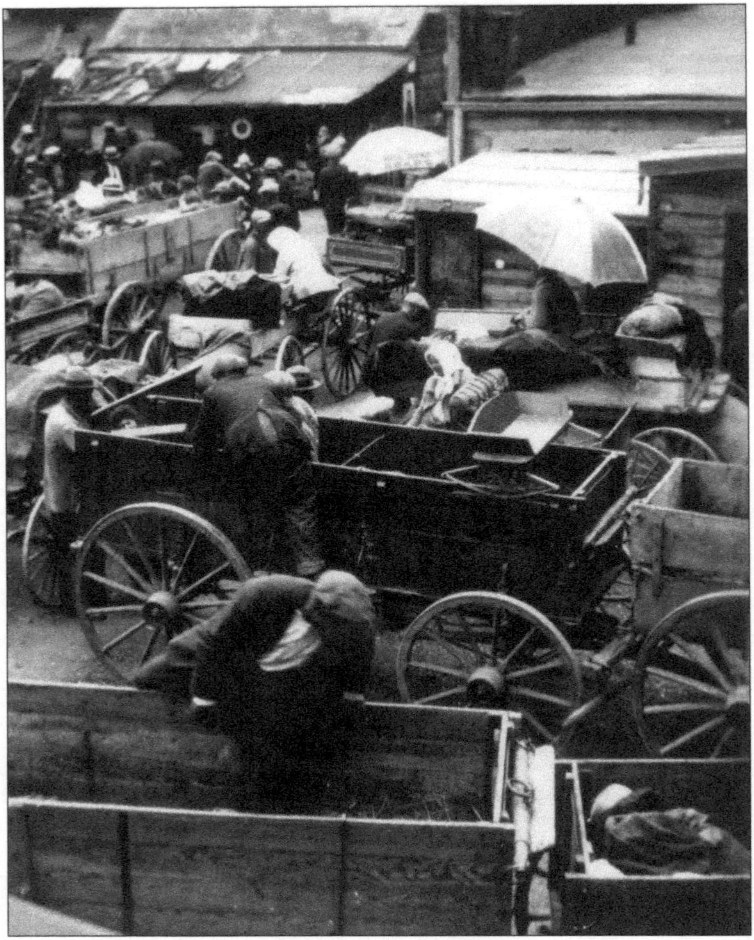

~

Behind the stalls of
the Public Market
young teamsters
up early
unloading wagons
take time
to unload
with me

~

When Grosney's wife
goes wild with rage

>   *Hoda —*
>   *You husband eater*
>   *Delilah*
>   *Whore!*

threatens to
expose me
to Daddy
I go crazy, too

>   *Who you*
>   *calling names?*

chase her
down Selkirk Street
out of earshot

But her fierceness
rouses me —

    What

            if

    he already

            knows

    then his

            trust

    can't be

            true

    and his

            silence

    is scarred

            shame

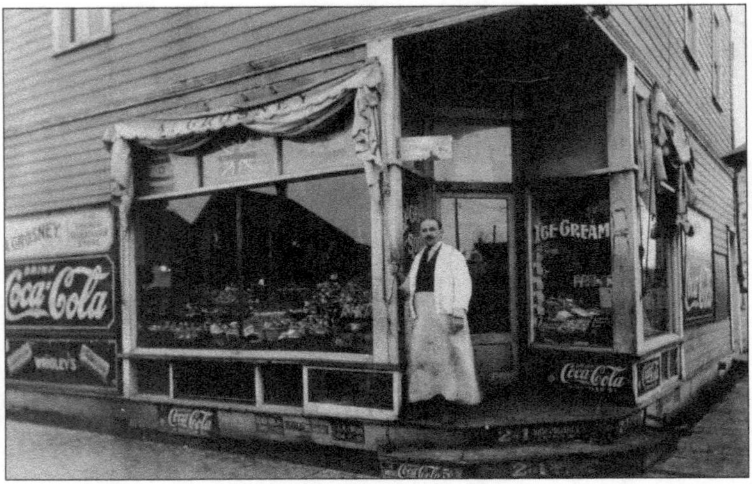
Coca-Cola
ICE-CREAM
Coca-Cola

~

Faith returns
in calmer moments

Daddy
> *his heart open*
> *his love pure*
doesn't know

he and I
still safe

~

I refuse relief
fend off visits
from government spies
sent to inspect
our draughty house
its buckled porch
prefer to manage
myself

What can a person do?

~

Dreams

of screaming
screaming
into the night
running wildly
through the streets

of retracing my steps
moving backward
in fear and panic
erasing the
trespass
of time

of shielding
my son
a guardian spirit
clutching his hand
feeding him sweets

Interlude III

Envelopes with cash
FOR THE PRINCE
sent to the Orphanage

Hoda's tithe
of guilt for
enduring debt

make a tidy sum
gifted to David
on his *Bar Mitzvah*

~

The first time
it bursts out of
him so fast
I pity the novice

close the door
once shagging
buddies leave
chat him up

> *No need to rush, you know*
> *Let's develop a little style*

Hands stroke
his back   chest
glide down
as

the
shards
of my being

enter
my son
whole

~

David departs
and madness
edges closer

its trace on my brow
its breath on my cheek
its tang on my tongue

And what should I do?
Close up shop?
Cross my legs and look virtuous?

>Who would soothe
>Daddy's throat with
>ginger tea and honey
>picnic with him
>in the park
>follow his stories of
>restless human impulse?

~

For as long as
his money lasts
the boy returns

I ache
in rejoining my son
and foreseeing his loss

~

I invite him
to visit
with Daddy
tell him
about Mamma

but great need
confuses the boy
foils my fantasy
of healing friendship

~

How do I do it? you ask
in disbelief.

    Yes, how?

    For the
    sins of
    loving and
    mothering
    God
    made and
    bound me
    whore
    to my son.

~

When I learn
from Gordie
he's gone
run away
   taken off
      disappeared
         beat it
            scrammed
               amscrayed
                  flit
I am bereft
this time
he's lost
for good

~

I am
this body –

ample enough
for ardent boys

soft enough
for seasoned men

strong enough
for my own son.

Its girth
gives me away

hides neither
joy nor sadness

marks me for life
for life makes me a mark.

VI: RENEWAL

~

For so long
I don't clue in –

>	Mr Minuk
>	pinching my backside
>	tossing me coins
>	as I scrub
>	his floor

>	Yankl
>	throwing me bones
>	and scraps
>	after I rub him
>	behind the deli counter

But now
with business
in full swing
I finally see –

>	They made me
>	who I am:
>	little orphan girl turned
>	North End whore

~

Time softens
Uncle Nate
who shuns
a bitter wife
indifferent sons
now claims us
as kin
visits regularly
drinks tea
with Daddy
tenders warmth
small bills
love's spare
change

~

Fornicate for Freedom!
I cry
and rail against
the war raging
in trenches
overseas
weep for
all boys
taken
lost or
missing

~

By war's end
my mattress
flattened
tossed
I've turned regular
show biz gal
now hostess of
Benjy Badner's
Delicatessen and Kibitzarnia
where nightly
with bells on
in sequins
I shake up
a party or two
boom laughter
over pinnacle   whist
corned beef on rye

~

Lazar
my Galician
finds his way
from Ukraine
to Benjy's
hangs around
every night
waits to walk
me home.

He likes my company
longs to talk
hear me tell
of North End life.

That's it —
just *chit chat*
more *chit chat*
through hushed
streets.

>	How is it
>	that's all
>	he wants?

He's survived
mass shootings
escaped the ovens
arrived here
from a DP camp.

> *All I need now*
>   he says
> *is your straight talk.*

~

An unlikely guide
Lazar leads me
softly through
suffering born
of deepest losses

        Mamma
        my newborn
        later grown son

toward light

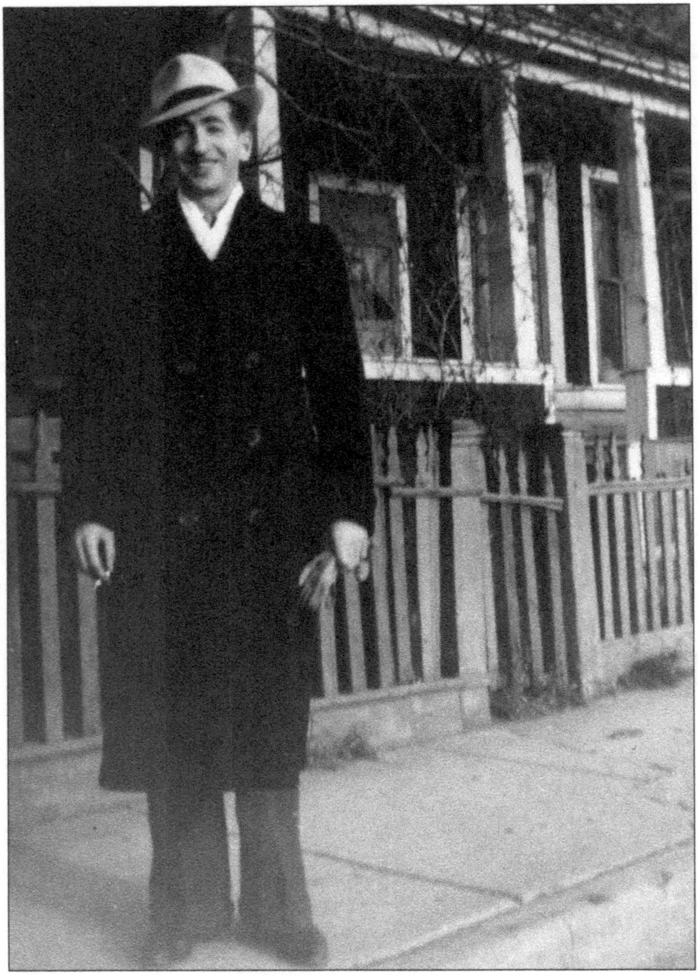

~

Story saves me –
Daddy's meandering
origin tale
bewildering
and beloved.

Why
had he survived
so much hardship –
the Czar's violence
terrible hatred
the plague
then poverty
humiliation
and loss?

> *To hold you*
> *Hodaleh –*
> *to see you*
> *grow and thrive*
> *here*
> *in safety*
> *and in love.*

His words
and will
strengthen
my resolve
against the
bullying torment
that rises anew
in Daddy's
hallowed
North End.

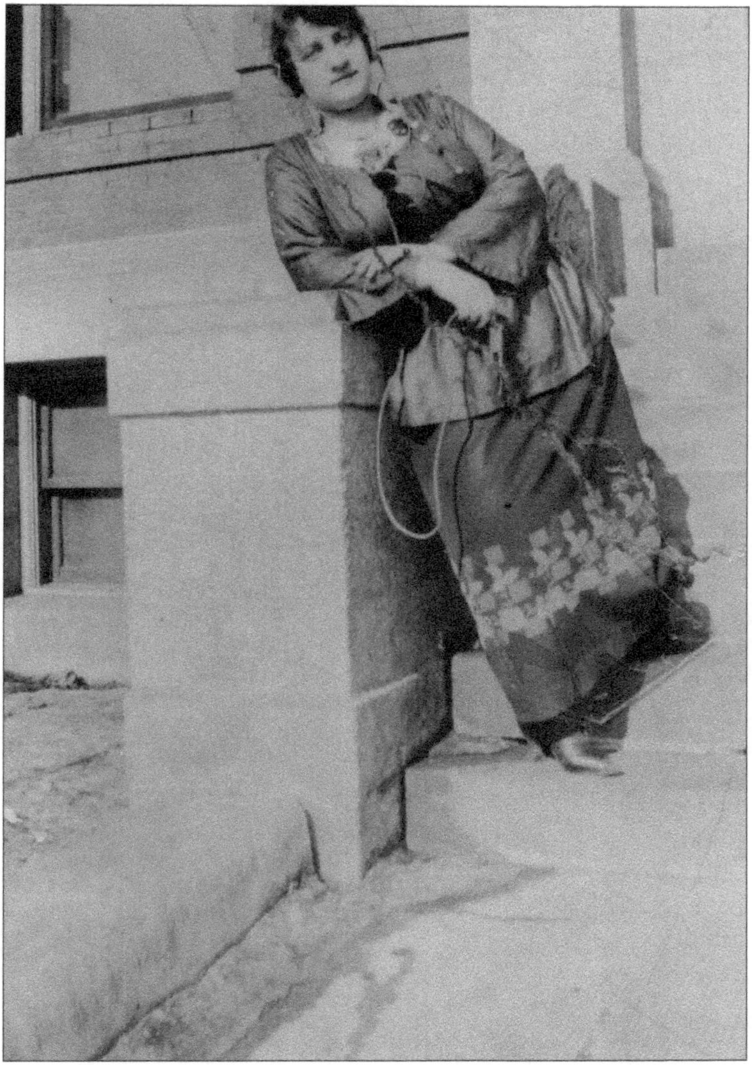

Coda

I bless this aging body
for it is sound

I curse this aging body
for it is weak

I embrace
its persistence

abhor
its flaps and folds

rely on
its strength

and deny
its force.

One day
I waken

to its will
and ken –

the body is guide
the body is guile

the body is grace
the body is mine.

> Homage to her body;
> found among Hoda's private papers

Notes

Proper nouns originate with Adele Wiseman's *Crackpot* (Toronto: McClelland and Stewart, 1974), with the exception of the following: Benjy Badner; Grosney; Dr Hershfeld; Mr Minuk; Mrs Minuk; Mrs Moroznick; Mount Carmel Clinic; St John's Technical High School; St Joseph's.

The following words belong to *Crackpot*: vulgar; meat scraps; fatso; cow; cracked; nuts; whore; watermelon; classy meatballs; gang shag; revolutionary; lump; unload; Bar Mitzvah; shards; run away; husband eater; taken off; disappeared; beat it; scrammed; amscrayed; flit; show biz.

The following phrases belong to *Crackpot:* run, Hoda, run; Hoda weighs a ton; I love you I love you I love you; take it away; tearing insides; what did I do; take good care of a prince in disguise; Hoda's not feeling so hot; it's my time of the month; forget it; worried about the clap; maybe a little bit pregnant; oh, I make ends meet; who you calling names; for the prince; develop a little style; close up shop; cross my legs and look virtuous; fornicate for freedom.

Illustrations

Front cover	Jewish Heritage Centre of Western Canada
Back cover	Archives of Manitoba
Page 3	Archives of Manitoba
Page 25	Jewish Heritage Centre of Western Canada
Page 28	Jewish Heritage Centre of Western Canada
Page 34	Archives of Manitoba
Page 38	Jewish Heritage Centre of Western Canada
Page 40	Jewish Heritage Centre of Western Canada
Page 50	Jewish Heritage Centre of Western Canada
Page 53	Jewish Heritage Centre of Western Canada
Page 67	Jewish Heritage Centre of Western Canada
Page 74	Jewish Heritage Centre of Western Canada
Page 77	Jewish Heritage Centre of Western Canada
Page 80	Jewish Heritage Centre of Western Canada
Page 84	Jewish Heritage Centre of Western Canada
Page 97	Jewish Heritage Centre of Western Canada
Page 106	Jewish Heritage Centre of Western Canada
Page 109	Jewish Heritage Centre of Western Canada

Acknowledgements

As I wrote this work, a number of people offered invaluable guidance. Early on, Lauren Kirshner urged me to forge ahead with this project and gave me the courage to do so. Merle Nudelman's perceptive comments helped me locate Hoda's voice. Sarah Henstra asked probing and incisive questions. And Dale Smith's poetic vision led me to refine my work. I am also indebted to publisher Luciana Ricciutelli for her vital encouragement and to Sholeh Sharifi for formatting the photographs included in this volume.

This book has benefited from the knowledge and assistance provided by Stan Carbone and Andrew Morrison of the Jewish Heritage Centre of Western Canada; Linda Eddy, Lewis St George Stubbs, and Shelley Sweeney of Archives and Special Collections, Elizabeth Dafoe Library, University of Manitoba; and the staff of the Archives of Manitoba and the City of Winnipeg Archives. This project was undertaken with the generous financial support of a Hadassah-Brandeis Institute Research Award and a Ryerson University Creative Fund Grant.

Ruth Panofsky is an award-winning poet who lives and writes in Toronto, where she teaches Canadian Literature and Culture at Ryerson University. She is the author of *Lifeline* (2001) and *Laike and Nahum: A Poem in Two Voices* (2007), which won the Helen and Stan Vine Canadian Jewish Book Award. *Radiant Shards: Hoda's North End Poems,* her third volume of verse, received a Hadassah-Brandeis Institute Research Award.